Political Verses And Curses

Political Verses And Curses

By
Mark H. Glissmeyer

Gradina Books

This book imitates a work of historical fiction. Any resemblance to actual persons, living or dead, should just be forgotten.

Copyright © 2019 by Mark H. Glissmeyer

All rights reserved.

No part of this book may be reproduced, or stored in a retrieval system, or transmitted in any form or by any means, electronic, mechanical, recording, photocopying, or otherwise, without the express written consent of the publisher.

ISBN-13: 978-0-9985416-5-5

Political Dedication:

This book is dedicated to the mistakes
That every generation always makes.

Danger:

If you trust a politician
You could need a mortician.

So strange was the life of Obama
He was born on the back of a llama
And while sporting a perm
He won a new term
So the Republicans cried to their mamma.

Hillary's emails were lost from a server
That's why they all made such a fervor
Some yelled for her tail
And life without bail
While the government tried to preserve her.

Presidential Priorities:

Why when they're elected today
Do Presidents just golf it away?

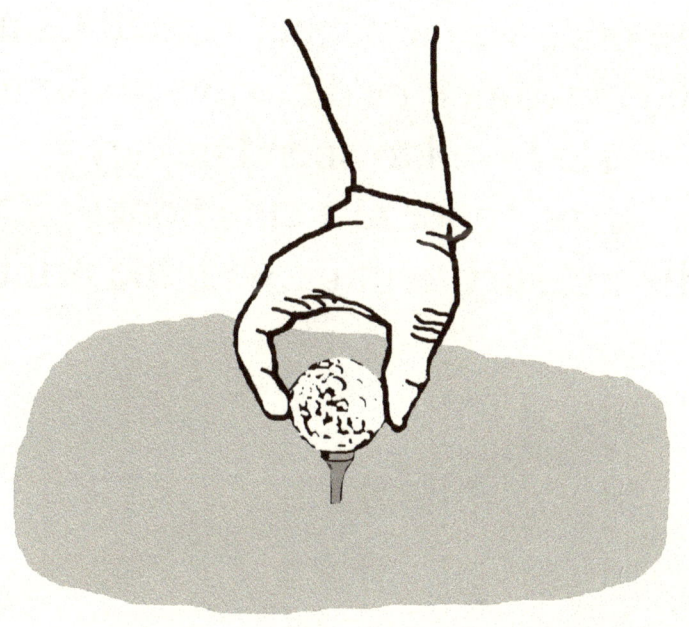

Mr. President, how many mulligans are you going to take on this tee?

There once was a winner named Clinton
Who at women he'd always go hinton
    He loved to spend money
    And squeeze a cute honey
While treasury kept up with the printon.

When ducks all fly north from their coup
They pass ponds all full of black goop
And if any should land
In the filthy oil sands
What's left won't make much of a soup.

Question:

If this book isn't funny
Do you want back your money?

How badly have things gone for Trump
With the media all watching his rump
They looked in his hole
And hired a mole
To keep his campaign in a slump.

Political Tell Alls:

They behave like hungry old crooks
But people keep buying their books.

HEADLINE NEWS

Another politician signs a $20 million book contract today

Dukakis once rode in a tank
But polling went bad as he sank
The helmet didn't fit
And his little pants split
Finally losing with no one to thank.

Question:

When you get to the end
Will you still be my friend?

The one who resigned was called Nixon
For trying to hide with the fix in
It could have been jail
For recording his trail
Like the lines left by old Mason Dixon.

Political Speeches:

When they end with a cry
You know it's a lie.

When I saw the ol' face of Gerald Ford
It reminded me of one crooked board
It never nailed straight
And squeaked like a gate
No wonder his wife always snored.

Political Promises:

If I had a dollar for every promise told
My house would be filled up with gold.

$1,345,765,654,365 in promises so far.

Energy policy:

What's up with that new solar power
It works well til it rains like a shower.

What happened to the power, honey? Is it raining again?

We once had a war in Iraq
That started with one big attack
But slowly by day
It whittled away
Until Saddam was placed in a sack.

Mission accomplished!

Economic Theory:

They say things will all trickle down
But it works like a watch never wound.

Have you seen the very large towers
Where people use wind to make power?
It won't care of their gender
As it spins like a blender
And chops up the birds into flour.

Plea Agreement:

If my words don't cause a slight smile
Please don't sue and take it to trial.

Case closed.

Have you ever heard of ol' Bernie Sanders
Who screams and sways as he panders?
His hair is a mess
Like a nut playing chess
Don't laugh when you just take a gander.

Tradition:

We always respect the First Lady
Regardless if her husband is shady.

Suggestion:

If this book seems awfully short
Then afterwords go have a snort.

Refreshments are on the house.

Political Caution:

Don't trust whatever they'll yap
And end up resembling a sap.

Political Demographics:

Either red states or blue states
They'll treat us like primates.

Does anyone remember Bob Dole
And how losing had taken its toll?
It caused a big wart
And shrunk him so short
He eventually looked like a troll.

I'm guessing that nobody notices me...

Question:

Is my rhyming so dumb
Am I worse than a bum?

Campaign Contributions:

To advance your vocations
Just sneak them donations.

That's not enough cash, we need more.

If you ever see old Jimmy Carter
Still wearing his pink and red garter
Don't mind if he grouses
While building new houses
Just maybe he'll end up a martyr.

Keep hammering Jimmy.

Watch what they do at our border
When they can't keep people in order
Just build the damn wall
Which needs to be tall
And be sure to use plenty of mortar.

Obama once went by Durango
To buy a small fruit called a mango
But he never got there
If anyone cared
He ended up dancing the tango.

HEADLINE NEWS

President Obama dances the Tango at the Argentina State Dinner

Question:

If you've read it this far
Can I light a cigar?

So close was Al Gore to George Bush
That the courts wanted voters to shush
Then just by a chad
Al was left mad
With a headache and tiny sore tush.

Caution:

Politics gets played in the gutter
But routinely gets milked like an udder.

When Dan Quayle went off to a school
He ended up becoming a fool
He couldn't spell potato
Then became a tomato
Before falling off the back of his stool.

I'll never forget how to spell that word again.

Question:

If this book was the worst ever penned
Will my body be needing a mend?

As Bush gave out lots of instructions
To find those darn weapons of destruction
So we started a war
And searched till we're sore
But never found a part from production.

Oddity:

Some Republicans get labeled as rhino's
If you wonder what it means
How would I know?

From all of the storms that keep forming
They created the scam global warming?
Yet someday they'll know
When we still get some snow
And the bees are buzzing while swarming.

Why anyone trusted Ronald Reagan
When he was constantly helped by a pagan
She kept following Mars
And reading his stars
Like those written by the late Carl Sagan.

They promised us plastic would save trees
So we switched over things in a breeze
But like some were afraid
It would never degrade
And now it all floats in the seas.

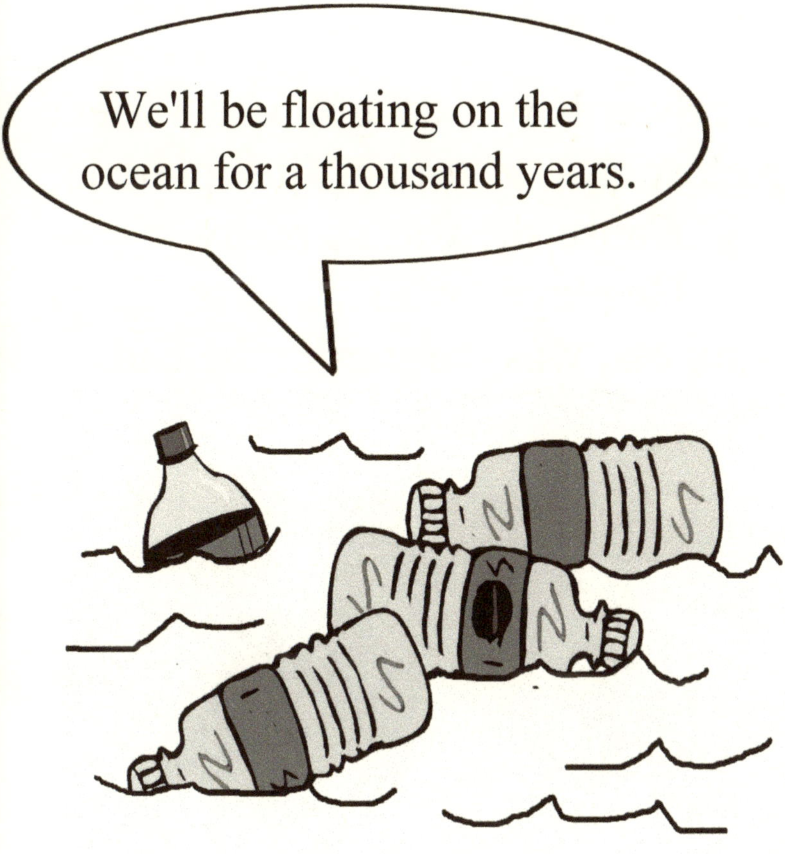
We'll be floating on the ocean for a thousand years.

John Edwards was caught with a friend
So close that he couldn't just pretend
Cause she was so pretty
He played with her kitty
And that was the start of the end.

That's not the kitty I played with!

Economic Theory:

One side likes to use tax and spend
But when will the costs ever end?

When logging was stopped by an owl
The foresters all cried it's a foul
But when they read the retort
It's now knotted in court
Until one side throws in the towel.

Public Union Power:

If it's the start of another school year
Then the teachers will strike without fear.

Declaration:

If the crooks in this book aren't fictitious
At least I'll admit that I'd wished it.

In the Gulf when a well blew apart
The spill was ignored from the start
    Cause nobody knew
    What they needed to do
Like a lost person left reading a chart.

HEADLINE NEWS

The President went golfing today while the spill at the oil well continued

As the Boy Scouts became too political
You knew things were getting quite critical
Then they added in girls
And others with curls
So everyone became analytical.

It's too bad what became of John Kerry
When he ran like a drowning canary
He knew they wouldn't vote
Cause he drove a swift boat
And pretended his service was scary.

So they finally legalized pot
It might be real good, is it not
And it may be a medicine
Smoked by Thomas Edison
Let's hope that our minds never rot.

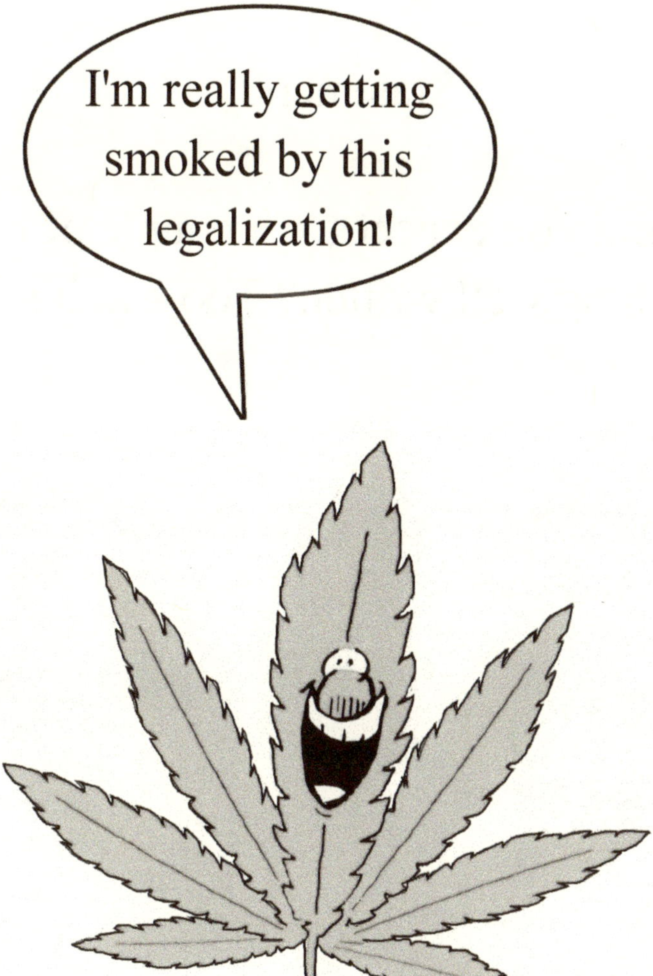
I'm really getting smoked by this legalization!

Statement:

What did you expect for a couple of bucks
Something well written? Too bad it sucks.

It was heartbreak when ol' President Bush
Threw up in Japan with a swoosh
While eating a banquet
They asked for a blanket
To clean up what flew on his tush.

He also made quite a yucky mess on the Prime Minister of Japan.

Thankfully no one was hurt
After Hawaii's wrong missile alert
The governor couldn't twitter
Which made residents bitter
And caused him to dance in a skirt.

HEADLINE NEWS

It was a false alarm in Hawaii when a ballistic missle alert was sent to residents accidentally...

It's time that we end this long scheme
Cause my rhyming is just out of steam.

Finis.

www.ingramcontent.com/pod-product-compliance
Lightning Source LLC
Chambersburg PA
CBHW021955090426
42811CB00001B/44